REPORT

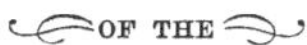

OF THE

HON. MARK D. WILBER,

CHAIRMAN OF THE COMMITTEE ON CITIES AND VILLAGES,

TO THE

SENATE OF MICHIGAN,

ON

THE DETROIT PARK BILL,

MARCH 5, 1873.

DETROIT:
DAILY POST BOOK AND JOB PRINTING ESTABLISHMENT.

1873.

REPORT

OF THE

Hon. MARK D. WILBER,

CHAIRMAN OF THE COMMITTEE ON CITIES AND VILLAGES,

TO THE

SENATE OF MICHIGAN,

ON

THE DETROIT PARK BILL,

MARCH 5, 1873.

DETROIT:
DAILY POST BOOK AND JOB PRINTING ESTABLISHMENT.
1873.

REPORT.

IN SENATE, LANSING, March 5, 1873.

THE committee on cities and villages, to whom was referred House Bill No. 69, entitled a Bill to amend an act entitled "An act supplementary to the charter of the city of Detroit, relating to a public park or other public grounds for the use of said city," being act No. 277 of the session laws of the year 1871, approved April 15, 1871,

Respectfully report, that in January, 1871, certain leading citizens of Detroit issued a call for a meeting "to consider the expediency of purchasing grounds for a public park."

The call stated that "the importance of securing lands for a public park cannot well be over estimated, as such grounds can be secured now cheaper than at any future time."

The meeting was held on the evening of January 24, 1871, when a committee was appointed "to propose and report a plan."

"On the 1st of February this committee made a report to a very large meeting. The substance of the report was that the Legislature, then in session, should be asked to pass a law providing for the appointment of a Board of Park Commissioners, whose duty it should be to select grounds for a park or boulevard, within or without the city limits, and to acquire such land after the means have been provided by the common council and a citizens' meeting."

At this meeting the report of the committee was adopted without change, and a new committee appointed, by whom "the meeting directed the reported plan to be embodied in the form of a bill, and submitted for enactment to the Legislature, then in session. The result was the Park Act passed April 15th, 1871. See Laws 1871, vol. 2, p. 1325.

The act of 1871 created a commission or board consisting of six persons. The board of commissioners were "vested with full power and authority to adopt plans for a public park or boulevard," and "to select and acquire the lands needful for such purposes;" conditional, however, "upon the ratification of such purchase by the common council, and the vote of a citizens' meeting." The park commission was duly organized, and immediately invited proposals of land suitable for a public park. Every site offered was carefully examined, and finally the commission selected a most eligible site, and entered into conditional contracts for the same on the most favorable terms.

"On December 8, 1871, the common council, by a vote of 16 ayes to 4 noes, approved the report of the commissioners, and ordered the proposition for the issue of the bonds necessary to complete the purchase to be submitted to a citizens' meeting.

"This action was vetoed by Mayor W. W. Wheaton, but on December 19, the council passed the resolution over the veto by a vote of 15 to 5."

After this final vote of approval by the common council, the commission, as the act required, called a meeting of the citizens to ratify their report. This meeting was held at the circuit court room; but was controlled, and finally broken up, through the influence of persons whose conduct your committee do not deem it necessary here to describe.

A second citizens' meeting, called for the same purpose, was held May 2d, 1872, which, though not as discreditable as the first, was nevertheless so conducted as to defeat its purpose. These several attempts convinced the commissioners that the city had outlived the period, as it had outgrown in numbers, the time when these once popular assemblages were practicably useful, and the "citizens' meeting" was, therefore, from necessity for this purpose, abandoned. With this failure to execute the plans adopted, according to the various conditions of the act, the commissioners were compelled either to abandon further attempt, or to seek and obtain relief from a higher source. To this end the commissioners addressed to the Legislature a memorial, reviewing the original defective act, and "asking that the law may be so amended as to give the commissioners the power necessary to secure a park for the city of Detroit." Upon this the "bill," which is the subject of your committee's report, was introduced into the House of Representatives, and passed. The passage of the bill has been warmly supported, as well as vigorously resisted.

Your committee have listened to several eloquent and learned discussions, both for and against the bill. In these arguments various and important issues were raised, as to-wit: Whether the city needs a "public park," and if so, whether it should have two or three parks, including a boulevard—the area sufficient for a park—its, or their location—the principle of assessment known as "benefits and damages"—the power of the Legislature to regulate and control municipal governments, and the proper exercise of its powers in authorizing compulsory taxation, without the consent of the tax-payers, for public projects not deemed "public necessities," in violation of ancient municipal customs. Upon these several issues, your committee, after hearing counsel, advocates, and citizens,—after visiting Detroit and examining with care the proposed park locations, their topography, characteristics, and surroundings, with a view to the prospective needs of a large, wealthy, and rapidly increasing commercial city,—find and submit:

That public parks for large cities are not mere pleasure grounds, and costly public luxuries, but public necessities. Their utility has been recognized through all the ages of civilization, as shown by all the large cities in every land. The public health, moral as well as physical, requires them,—every principle of sanitary law demands them. The poor, the sick, and the children cry out for them. The prolonged existence of the thousands who are born, live, die, and are buried within the walls or limits of large towns, depends upon these "public lungs." The millions that people our great cities cannot each have the costly private grounds, nor even the simple "door yard" and garden, but all may have, own, and enjoy in common one still grander and better, a public "door yard" and garden, towards which the doors of the whole city open—a park for the parent, and a play-ground for the children of *all*.

The uses and purposes of a public park are grand and comprehensive in their scope, and far reaching in their benefits. It becomes of necessity a public educator. Visitors at Central Park see admirably illustrated the use of money in the hands of men of genius and taste, used in instructing the public in the art of landscape gardening, as taught in older lands. Yet, as an educator, Central Park is still far behind many of the parks of Europe. Their zoological gardens—conservatories of exotics—their tropical gardens, their aquaria, representing sections of the seas, with their fishes, animals, shells, corals, anemone—in a word, the wonders of the world as found in their native element—their museums of natural history, botany, geology, mineralogy, etc., are almost unknown to American parks.

The "Garden of Plants," in Paris, contains the forest and fruit trees, the shrubs and flowers, almost, of the world. Each has attached a small tin label, on which is written its name, country and use. Thus, a tree, shrub, or plant with a white label shows that in fruit, leaf, flower, bark, root, or juice it is food-producing. The blue label indicates its extracts are used in some form in the arts as a coloring, ink or dye. Those with yellow label are medicinal; the black poisonous; the red ornamental, etc. Here tens of thousands receive free that which Americans would destroy—the surplus shrubs, plants, slips, grafts, roots, seeds, etc., for their private homes and gardens, and instruction in their culture. All this can be had and practiced in any park, with scarce an added cost.

The park is also a school of art. In our country, where the law of primogeniture does not obtain, private parks of any extent are the exception; hence, the public park must be the high school, where students in "landscape gardening" are to receive instruction from the hand of a master. Parks are pictures; aye, whole galleries of paintings, where nature comes, with the pencil of spring, and summer, and autumn; of bud, and flower, and fruit, of sunlight and shadow, to execute the design of man's imagination.

America has but begun to take lessons in the art of picture-making with tree, fruit and flower, lakelet, lawn aud fountain;

indeed, only such as the gardens of Versailles or Potsdam give a just conception of how beautiful and how instructive these can be made. The park, therefore, becomes the "Academy of Design" for the city and the State. Here are the originals from a master's hand. With such institutions of learning in our cities, where all may enter and graduate, you will soon find the people here, as in Europe, copying to embellish their own homes.

The locating of one for the present, rather than two or three parks and a boulevard, considering the amount of money to be appropriated, and the present population of the city, is believed to have been wise. The sum named in the act to purchase grounds, with the annual sum for their improvement and care, is not too great for one park, in size and arrangement creditable to such a city.

Upon the question of area, and access, the experience of other cities cannot but be profitable. New York city has eighteen public parks and squares, amounting to one acre in fourteen of the whole island, besides quite an area of private grounds and those belonging to State and city asylums and institutions, not open to the public. Central Park contains 844 acres. It is in the form of a parallelogram, the narrowness of which necessitated the expenditure of several millions to create artificial hills and valleys, so that in following its labyrinth of carriage drives, bridle paths, and walks, the illusion of immense areas should be preserved. New York should have, and desired much greater areage, but her limited island space, unlike almost all other cities, forbid it. "Prospect Park," in Brooklyn, occupies the finest park location in the world. It is larger than Central Park. Convenience of access, however, was sacrificed to its other desired advantages.

Philadelphia had many fine squares and parks, including Fairmount. Her citizens, thoroughly appreciating the great need of parks for a manufacturing population, already the largest in the world, and failing to find sufficient and suitable space within the city limits, crossed the Schuylkill, opposite Fairmount, where they laid out and are completing a park in size truly imperial, it having been enlarged by the present Legislature of Pennsylvania to 2,700 acres. Baltimore, Washington, Chicago, Buffalo, and all the cities of New England, indeed, nearly every American city, has its parks among its proudest monuments, as well as useful and beneficent public works. Even our Nation has its parks—"The Valley of the Yosemite" and the "Yellowstone." "National Parks" are not limited to acres numbered by hundreds, but by hundreds of square miles, filled with objects such as only God can carve, and plant, and water. The cities of Europe are also largely supplied with public parks. The "Phœnix Park," of Dublin, contains 1,752 acres. "Calton Hill," "Princess Gardens," the Castle grounds, those of "Holyrood," "Arthur's Seat," and "Salisbury Crags," in and adjoining Edinburgh, occupy spaces united as large as the entire city besides. In the arguments before the committee, statements were made giving the small sizes of the London Parks, as follows:

St. James Park,	59 acres
Green Park,	55 acres
Buckingham Palace Gardens,	50 acres
Hyde Park,	389 acres
Kensington Park,	35 acres
Kensington Gardens,	262 acres

But the fact was omitted that all these are almost in one body, 850 acres—a mere chain of parks, separated or broken only in their continuity by two or three short avenues, unoccupied by buildings. Besides these, London has within its limits numerous other parks and places, including Regent's, 473 acres; Victoria, 248 acres; Greenwich, 185 acres; Battersea, 175 acres—with 1,200 acres in parks of lesser size—being considerably above 3,000 acres within the city—while in her suburbs are found Windsor, 3,800 acres; Hampton Court, 1,842 acres; Richmond, 2,468 acres; Kew, 648 acres; Sydenham, 200 acres—making, with some smaller ones, over 10,000 acres more; added to these are the parks of several noblemen, all used and frequented by great masses of the citizens of the metropolis.

London therefore has opened to her 3,500,000 people greater comparative park accommodations than a new park covering 450 acres would afford the 100,000 of Detroit. Paris includes within its fortifications 12 or 15 elegant parks and gardens, but the

"Bois de Boulogne," her central park, containing 2,150 acres is entirely outside the fortifications. The park at St. Cloud is beyond the "Bois de Boulogne" and across the Seine. Versailles is 11 miles distant, the forest of Fontainbleau, 60 miles in circumference, is 40 miles distant, yet these and several other large parks within the same limits are daily frequented by the millions of Paris. The "Thier Garten" of Berlin extends for several miles, and is adjoining, but entirely outside the city's gates. The park history, however, of any one of these old towns is substantially the history of all.

The location of the Detroit park by the commissioners was perhaps the most delicate and difficult question presented for their solution. Several sites were named to the board, but four only were reported upon by them. Below the city on the river they failed to obtain any considerable quantity of land, and had land sufficient been offered, the gravest objections were presented by the fact that the proposed site was already cut by two great thoroughfares and one railway. The second proposed site, that upon the Grand River road, and the third, upon the Pontiac road, or Woodward avenue site, are subject to quite the same objections. They are more remote than that of Hamtramck from the population centers of the city, the lands are unbroken plateaus, entirely wanting in those topographical conditions so desirable for the purpose required. The soil is clay and not well adapted to garden purposes. The routes to these sites lie over three constructed and one located railway line, which cross the avenues on a level, and over which it is estimated there will soon pass a train every five minutes, making the drive extremely dangerous.

The Hamtramck site, the one chosen by the Board, is above the city on the river, three miles from the city hall. It has a river frontage of 1,300 feet, or about one-fourth of a mile.

This affords not only a sufficient water approach, but admits of a very considerable river drive, and promenade. A portion of these lands next the river are low and admirably adapted in their improvement, to the construction, at slight expense, of artificial lakes, a most desirable adjunct to a park, for boating, sailing, and skating, combining as they do the element of safety, to all seeking this union of health and pleasure. The main portion of these lands rises to a considerable altitude above the river, the highest, it is believed, in the vicinity of the city. This elevation "commands a view of the city, of the Canada shore, of Belle Isle, and an unsurpassed water view, extending far into Lake St. Clair. During the season of navigation, save in the Bay of New York, so animated a water view is nowhere else to be seen in this country. It may not be generally known that the vessel tonnage that passes through the Detroit river exceeds the whole tonnage of the United States employed in foreign commerce. By actual count made a few years ago, it was found that about *twenty-three thousand* water craft passed the light houses on the St. Clair Flats in a single season.

About 300 acres of this land is forest and second-growth woodland, an almost invaluable consideration, Nature having already made it what otherwise would have cost years of time and great expense. This wood shades a long, deep, irregular ravine, broad enough in the bottom for a carriage-way—with sloping sides for walks, rustic seats and bridges, grottoes, waterfalls, and every method of adornment peculiar to the art of landscape gardening. There are several kinds of soil, but the largest portion is a sandy loam, valuable for roads and walks, as well as park culture.

Another important fact associated with this location, and with no other proposed site, is its half isolated position, occupying as it does, lands jutting out into, or between the river and Lake St. Clair, and outside the line of commercial traffic. It is not now, and never will be, traversed by any great railway or highway. Even Jefferson avenue is so situated in its passage across this site, as to admit of the park being entirely separate and exclusive. All drives, walks and bridle paths can be carried under the avenue, so as to admit the freest and most unobstructed communication, from one part to the other. A city railway already runs to the entrance of these grounds—they having been chosen long since, as the best adapted in the suburbs of the city, for a "driving park" and "fair purposes." As a matter of general access, the principal approach in summer will be the river. The city, as now built, stretches its length along the river a distance twice to four times its depth. The mass of citizens live, therefore, at short distances from the steamer highway. In summer boats will run with great frequency, and at half car fares, giving a delightful sail and the pure air of the straits, as added benefits and pleasures to a park visit. The park dock would also be used for landing material required in the improvement of the park, and in building the new water works and reservoirs, saving, as compared with the cost of transportation to an inland site, sums, in the course of years, greatly lessening the cost of these works. The principle of assessments, known as benefits and damages, is one that merits the most careful consideration. This does not, however, appear a popular doctrine in this State. At the same time, it has been very equitably and practically met in this case. First, the lands have been offered in contract, to the park commissioners, for a park, at prices far below their market value. Second, parties owning adjoining property have subscribed $18,000 with which to purchase 300 feet additional river front, to be donated to the city for park purposes. In addition to the foregoing, the territory surrounding the proposed park shall, by the terms of the act, be annexed to the city before its provisions are enforced or executed. This territory has already upon it residences and manufactories worth from one to two millions; all this must be taxed at once for its proportion of the expenses of the city government, together with the city's present indebtedness. In the argument heard, it was claimed that by the location of the park the adjoining lands would not be increased in value. This cannot be correct. That the effect upon valuations will be the same upon the location of this, as universally obtains in the location of parks in other towns, is believed. The surrounding property would then be appreciated to double or quadruple its present value, and increase relatively the amount of taxes produced by it.

The statement that the mere location of the park, without its improvement, will not result in increased values, is also a fallacy. The *fact alone* that the park has been legally located will *at once* double the price, and hence, assessed value of the surrounding property. The city has now, practically, no public grounds for the people. Locate the Hamtramck park, open it to the public on the avenue and river front, bring it within the control and protection of the city police, and its driving-course, its open spaces for "ball clubs" and drill grounds, its 300 acres of forest and woodland, its pure air, its extended views, its rural charms and natural attractions, alone, without the expenditure of a dollar in imwrovement, will make it at once the popular resort of the people.

For the first, then, in its history will the city have provided grounds dedicated to the use of the public, where, henceforth, the picnic party, the public and Sunday schools, all the children who work or study, can go and breathe the pure air, and gather instruction from the trees, birds, flowers, river, lake, and rivulet—God's tutors—too much neglected by the over-worked, over-studied, over-crowded children of our cities.

The area included in the proposed annexed territory, exclusive of the park, is about 3,000 acres. This, with its factories and buildings, is estimated at $2,000,000, which, long before the maturity of the bonds would equal $20,000,000. The assessed valuation of property in Detroit is about 40 per cent. of its real value. Forty per cent. of $20,000,000 equals $8,000,000. This at one per cent., which is less than the city tax, would yield $80,000 per annum, which will pay the $50,000 annual appropriation for park improvement, together with $30,000 interest on $300,000 park bonds,—leaving in fact no cost whatever to be charged to the city, and taxed upon either rich or poor; giving them a park at the expense of those owning property in its vicinity. True, there will be city expenses upon this new territory, but this will be largely met by its growing population. It will not be forgotten that the water board propose taking for the city, by an arrangement with the park commission, a considerable portion of the park grounds, on which to erect the new city reservoirs. The cost of these lands, charged to the water board, will materially lessen the original cost, interest, and maintenance accounts properly charged to the park.

The constitutional and legal principles involved in the issue as to "the powers of the Legislature to regulate, and control municipal governments, and the proper exercise of its powers in authorizing compulsory taxation, without the consent of the tax-payer, for public projects not deemed public necessities," the committee believe to be too well settled, to require any elaborate opinion.

An act of the Legislature is the exercise of the highest authority that the State exercises upon earth; or, as Blackstone says, "The act of Parliament is the exercise of the highest authority that the kingdom exercises upon earth."

"Municipalities must look to the State for such charters of government as the Legislature shall see fit to provide." "The creation of municipal corporations, and the conferring upon them of certain powers, and subjecting them to corresponding duties, does not deprive the Legislature of the State of that complete control over their citizens which was before possessed." "It still has authority to amend their charters, enlarge or diminish their powers, extend or limit their boundaries, over-rule their action whenever it is deemed unwise, impolitic, or unjust, and even abolish them altogether in the legislative discretion."—*Cooley's Con. Lim.*, 191, 192, and numerous cases there cited.

Upon the question of taxation the following case is deemed conclusive:

In People vs. Mahoney, 13 Mich., 500, where the Metropolitan Police act of Detroit was attacked, the court said: "The taxation under the act, it is said, is really in the hands of a police board, a body in the choice of which the people of Detroit have no voice.' This argument is one which might be pressed upon the legislative department with great force, if it were true in point of fact. But as the people of Detroit are really represented throughout, the difficulty suggested can hardly be regarded as fundamental. They were represented in the Legislature which passed the act, and had the same proportionate voice there with the other municipalities in the State, all of which receive from that body their powers of local government, and such only as its wisdom shall prescribe within the constitutional limit. They were represented in that body when the present police board were appointed by it, and the Governor, who is hereafter to fill vacancies, will be chosen by the State at large, including their city. There is nothing in the maxim that taxation and representation go together which requires that the body paying the tax shall alone be consulted in its assessment; and if there were, we should find it violated at every turn in our system. The State Legislature not only has a control in this respect over inferior municipalities, which it exercises by general laws, but it sometimes finds it necessary to interpose its power in special cases to prevent unjust or burdensome taxation, as well as to compel the performance of a clear duty."

It is not the rule of government first to obtain the consent of the tax payer, before the passage of laws authorizing compulsory taxation. "The government provides court-houses, buildings for its seminaries of instruction, aqueducts to carry pure and wholesome water into large towns, etc., etc., and other measures of public utility, in which the public at large are interested, and which require the appropriation of private property." "Such, for instance, as the construction of a public park, which, in large cities, is as much a matter of public utility as a railway or a supply of pure water, or sewers of cities." *Cooley's Con. Lim., 533, 534;* also, *Matter of Central Park extension, 16 Abb. Pr. Rep. 55; Owners of Ground vs. Mayor, etc., of Albany, 15 Wend., 374,* and *Hildreth vs. Lowell, 11 Gray, 345.*

The original park act was passed in 1871, without opposition from Detroit, or other source.

"The principle is established that whenever a power is given by a statute, everything necessary to the making of it effectual, or required to attain the end, is implied." *II Kent. Com., 272.*

Men are comprehensive in their grasp of ideas, limited in their philosophies and faiths, generous in their charities, or the opposite, as they are educated in life, as their tutors, business and surroundings, are broad or narrow. America and her cities are no "pent up Uticas." Nor is Detroit pent up. It is growing with a healthy, strong, vigorous growth. Her public works should speak, if they speak at all, words worthy the metropolis of the Peninsulas. Seated, as she is, at the gate of the lakes, receiving court and tribute from a continent, her petition, bearing the names of so many whose intelligence, culture, wealth, rank, and public worth are written all over the city they builded, expresses a prayer that should be granted. Your committee therefore have directed me to report back the park bill favorably to the Senate, without amendment, and recommend its passage.

M. D. WILBER, *Chairman.*

www.ingramcontent.com/pod-product-compliance
Lightning Source LLC
LaVergne TN
LVHW020637110826
845149LV00004B/1252

* 9 7 8 1 4 1 8 1 9 1 2 6 9 *